Bohemian Fa

A grayscale coloring book featuring 25 lovely ladies for you to color!

This coloring book features 25 single sided grayscale images taken from Molly's watercolor paintings of bohemian beauties and fantasy abstract portraits. This is not a typical line drawing coloring book; instead it features grayscale images showing the shading and highlights. Suitable mediums include markers, colored pencils, pastels, and gel pens. Not suitable for wet media. This coloring book is intended for older kids and grown ups.

MOLLY HARRISON
2015

Molly Harrison
2012

MOLLY HARRISON
2015

MOLLY HARRISON
5/2010

MOLLY HARRISON 2015

Molly Harrison 2015

Molly Harrison
2014

MOLLY HARRISON 2015

MOLLY HARRISON 2014

MOLLY HARRISON 2014

MOLLY HARRISON
2015

MOLLY HARRISON 2014

MOLLY HARRISON
2014

MOLLY HARRISON
2012

48923305R00031

Made in the USA
Middletown, DE
30 September 2017